FOODS JUST LIKE MINE (ONLY DIFFERENT)

Written by Eliza Nodes

KidHaven PUBLISHING

Published in 2026 by
KidHaven Publishing, an Imprint of Greenhaven Publishing, LLC
2544 Clinton St., Buffalo, NY 14224

Written by: Eliza Nodes
Edited by: Rebecca Phillips-Bartlett
Designed by: Amelia Harris

Cataloging-in-Publication Data
Names: Nodes, Eliza.
Title: Foods / Eliza Nodes.
Description: Buffalo, NY : KidHaven Publishing, 2026. | Series: Just like mine (only different) | Includes glossary and index.
Identifiers: ISBN 9781534551671 (pbk.) | ISBN 9781534551688 (library bound) | ISBN 9781534551695 (ebook)
Subjects: LCSH: Food--Juvenile literature. | Food habits--Juvenile literature.
Classification: LCC RA601.N634 2026 | DDC 641.3--dc23

Printed in China

CPSIA compliance information: Batch #QW26KH: For further information contact Greenhaven Publishing LLC at 1-844-317-7404.

Please visit our website, www.greenhavenpublishing.com. For a free color catalog of all our high-quality books, call toll free 1-844-317-7404 or fax 1-844-317-7405.

Find us on

Image Credits

Images courtesy of Shutterstock.com, unless otherwise stated.
Recurring – natnatnat, Irina Strelnikova. Cover – graficriver_icons_logo, tanghulu, onigiri, Rusne Pazdrazdyte, Indian Food Images, mayakova, margouillat photo, kiboka, Tim UR. 2–3 – Pressmaster. 4–5 – LightField Studios, oliveromg. 6–7 – India Picture, Pixel-Shot. 8–9 – Q88, Ika Rahma H, GoodStudio. 10–11 – Kleber Cordeiro, Juliana Verly. 12–13 – 88STOCKVN, duo369, float. 14–15 – Roman Samborskyi, graletta, Keith Homan. 16–17 – AJP, Image bug, nuwatphoto. 18–19 – Luis Molinero, perthstagedtosell, pakww, Cali6ro. 20–21 – Halfpoint, etorres. 22–23 – Sergii Kozii, Robert Kneschke.

CONTENTS

WORDS THAT LOOK LIKE THIS CAN BE FOUND IN THE GLOSSARY ON PAGE 24.

A LOOK AROUND THE CAFETERIA

At my school, everyone eats different things for lunch. Some people buy hot meals. Some people have packed lunches. The cafeteria always smells good!

My friends and I bring packed lunches to school. Some of the foods we eat are part of our cultures. Some people can only eat or only like certain foods.

MY LUNCH

I like to eat lots of different things. My parents put different things in my lunch box every day. This makes it interesting and fun for me when I open it at lunchtime.

Today's lunch has some of my favorite foods. I love fruit, so my parents have packed me some cherries, apricots, an orange, and a banana. I also have a sandwich and some rice cakes. Yummy!

HARU'S LUNCH

This is Haru. Haru's parents are from Japan. Haru brings his lunch to school in a bento box. A bento box is a small box split into sections.

Inside the bento box, each section contains a different part of the meal. Bento boxes contain rice or noodles. They usually have some vegetables and fish or meat inside.

SOFIA'S LUNCH

Sofia's family is from Brazil. Today, she has brought beans and rice to eat at lunchtime. Lots of people in Central and South America enjoy this meal.

Sofia's family recipe uses white rice and black beans. Today, she is having it with cooked chicken. Sofia says that this dish is a part of her cultural identity. She is very proud of this.

MEI'S LUNCH

For lunch, Mei sometimes has soup with xiaolongbao. The soup is made by cooking vegetables or meat in water. Xiaolongbao are steamed Chinese buns. They are filled with meat and broth.

Xiaolongbao are steamed in a bamboo basket until they are cooked. They are bite-sized buns, which makes them easy to eat. This is why some parents make them for their children's school lunch.

JAKE'S LUNCH

My friend Jake has to be careful with food. Jake is allergic to peanuts. Being allergic to something means his body has a harmful reaction to something that is safe for many people.

Jake cannot eat anything with peanuts in—even if it is only a small amount. These small amounts are called traces. Jake and his parents have to read food labels very carefully.

ABDUL'S LUNCH

Let's take a look at Abdul's lunch. Abdul brings his lunch to school in a tiffin box. A tiffin box is made up of four metal bowls stacked on top of one another.

Each bowl has a different part of the meal inside. This usually includes rice, curry, dhal, and roti. Dhal is made with lentils, and roti is a type of flatbread. Tiffin boxes help keep home-cooked lunches warm.

JULIET AND CHARLOTTE'S LUNCHES

My friend Juliet is vegetarian. Vegetarians do not eat meat or fish but do eat eggs and dairy products. Juliet is having a tofu wrap and yogurt for lunch.

My friend Charlotte is vegan. Vegans do not eat or use anything that comes from an animal. This includes meat, fish, dairy, eggs, and honey. Charlotte is having veggie nuggets and avocado and carrot sushi for lunch.

DARREN'S LUNCH

My friend Darren has to keep track of what and how much he eats. He has type 1 diabetes. This means his body does not make enough of something called insulin. Insulin is a hormone.

Darren has an insulin pump that gives his body insulin automatically. He wears a continuous glucose monitor, or CGM, on his arm. This measures his sugar levels. Today, Darren has pasta and salad in his lunch.

TIME FOR CLASS

It is the end of lunchtime. Now you have seen what my friends and I have for lunch. What do you and your friends have for lunch? How are your lunches different from one another's?

I love that my friends and I are so different from one another. We are unique, and the food we eat shows that. These differences make us interesting and amazing. It would be boring if we were all the same!

GLOSSARY

automatically	by itself without human control
broth	soup without anything solid in it
cultural identity	people's view of who they are in terms of their way of life, based on where they come from
cultures	the traditions, ideas, and ways of life of different groups of people
dairy	products that are made from milk, such as yogurt and cheese
epinephrine auto-injector	a device for getting a dose of adrenaline into the body to help with serious allergic reactions
hormone	a chemical in your body that tell parts of your body what to do
recipe	a set of steps that explain how to make a particular dish or meal
unique	unlike anything or anyone else

INDEX